Love By Choice

By Lucas Asu
and Franca Navarra

Table Of Contents

Dedication

This book is dedicated to everyone who believes in love.

Acknowledgement

We would like to acknowledge and thank all the inspiring teachers and coaches that have gone before us and have paved the path for us to continue expanding and engineering better insights, tools and strategies for building and growing a deeper level of love, passion and fulfillment in relationships. To them we are profoundly grateful.

Special thanks to Melissa Dann for editing this book.

Book Bonus

Thank you for purchasing *Love by Choice: The Ultimate Guide for Creating Your Dream Relationship* Book.

Don't Pass Up the Chance to Be a Winner!

As a 'Thank You' for your support, we have decided to enter every person who purchased the book into a special drawing for a full 60-minute private session with Lucas and Franca.

We will draw 2 winners who's name will be announced on our Facebook page as well as we will reach out personally via email.

Please enter your name and email on this page:

https://lovebychoice.mykajabi.com/p/bonus-private-session

Preface

You attracted this book *Love by Choice* because you are ready for a new level of insights about relationships and how to create your dream relationship. No matter how many times you have failed or been unlucky in having the relationship you know you truly deserve, this book will unlock a brand new love and relationship future for you. You can create and have your dream relationship.

This book is inspired out of our experiences working with thousands of couples and singles coaching and assisting them to transform the quality of their relationships. We began noticing that most of the challenges and problems couples have were identical, and their root causes were easily traceable. In this book we take you behind our master coach curtain and share the raw insights, leading-edge skills, tools, and strategies we use to transform those relationships and help individuals create their dream relationships. And, most importantly, to empower and equip them with the right tools to continuously grow and nurture their relationships through time.

The right relationship is the source of the deepest love, passion, joy, and fulfillment any human being can ever experience. So this book is really about how to create your dream and your ultimate relationship. We believe that the ultimate relationship starts with you developing and having that relationship with yourself first.

Chapter One explores how our environments and the relationships around us often shape and influence our own views and choices of love and relationships.

Chapter Two is about your relationship with you. This chapter is all about having a greater understanding of yourself and a greater relationship with yourself so you will be able to have an extraordinary relationship with someone else. You cannot give others that which you do not have. Love starts with you and love starts from you. You will learn how to create a deeper relationship with yourself.

Chapters Three and Four are about how to make the right relationship selection. You will learn the significance of making the right relationship selection. Your breakthrough will be discovering that it is the person you select to be in a relationship with that determines the quality and the destiny of your relationship. And it is this that will to a greater extent determine the quality of your life positively or negatively. When you make decisions to get into a relationship or marriage for any other reason other than true love as your primary reason, you will pay a severe price. And when your true intention is love and you make your selection from a very conscious place, then the love, passion, and fulfillment will be amazingly magical. You will learn insights as to how to make the right selection by gaining clarity about what you really want and what matters to you most in a relationship. You will also learn about selecting a lover with a personality that will complement who you are and not one that will put you both in constant conflict. You will learn the most common mistakes people make when selecting a relationship partner and how to avoid those mistakes.

Chapter Five is about the Six Needs of a Relationship: what everybody wants in a relationship. When you understand what these Needs are and you make it your responsibility to meet them at the highest level and assume your love also makes it his or her responsibility to fulfill them at the highest level, then you will have a relationship that will inspire others around you.

Chapter Six exposes you to the Six Stages of Love and Relationships. These stages will enable you to accurately and precisely measure the intensity of love, passion, and fulfillment in your relationship as well as know exactly whether the relationship is going up or downhill.

Chapter Seven is about getting a sound and firm grip on relationship communication skills and how to effectively communicate with your lover. Everyone, including your lover, has a unique style of communicating. Knowing this is crucial because it helps you to be able to get through to him or her in any situation. You will finally know how to have heartfelt communication with your lover. This chapter will also remove the communication blinders and for the first time you will understand how to communicate with anyone using their unique style or representational system.

The last chapter, Chapter Eight, is all about the seven skills of a relationship. These skills, as well as the accompanying strategies, are what you really need to not just start a relationship, but to be able to nurture and grow your relationship to make it delicious, extraordinary, magnificent, and lasting.

You can have the dream relationship you truly deserve. The power is in your heart. Allow yourself to have it.

We love you,

Franca Navarra and Lucas Asu

66 *The vast majority of people seeking love and relationships have bought into and suffer from the cultural belief that their better half is out there. This is a myth. Our culture continues to perpetuate this myth with the constant use of words such as "my better half," "my other half," or "my significant other." This presupposes that without this person in your life you are an incomplete person and you need them in order to make you whole. Here is your new truth from this day forward—no one can ever make you whole. You've got to know you are already whole.* 99

66 *The purpose of love is not to seek for someone to make you whole, but to share and intensify life experiences and emotions.* 99

66 *Those who seek relationships in order to find someone to make them whole will always end up in disappointment and frustration. Those that seek relationships in order to experience love, share experiences, growth, and contribute beyond themselves are the ones that will experience the deepest level of love, joy, and fulfillment.* 99

–Lucas Asu

Chapter

1

Your Early Programming and Experiences of Love

Greatly Influence Your Choices and Decisions of Love

(Case Study)

Franca: When I was a teenager I looked forward to someday meeting that boy who was going to sweep me off my feet and together we could experience the magic of love poets have so often talked about. My mind, like most girls and boys, was filled with the hope and expectation of the thrill of love, the ecstasy of a kiss, and the adventure of romance. But my environment and strict Italian and Catholic upbringing was teaching a constricted and narrowed view of love and life. Love was always negatively perceived. I heard numerous times beliefs such as "The purpose of love between a boy and a girl, a man and a woman, is to get married. Who you date is who you get married to. Sex outside of marriage is disobedience and a sin against God and will lead to eternal condemnation and damnation."

This was the gospel and distorted view of love I heard and saw growing up. But in my heart and within my being I knew love is the most intensely amazing feeling and experience anyone can ever feel. I knew love is one of mankind's greatest gifts; the gift of loving and being loved. What I knew within and believed love is and what I saw and heard around me were two different realities. Love was not a subject my mom and dad ever wanted to openly talk about. They were uncomfortable and sometimes awkward whenever I asked a question regarding love, relationships, or sex. Can you relate?

Your Frame of References Shape Your Relationship Choices

When I turned eighteen, I had to rely upon those same limited beliefs, limited frames of references and early programming in making choices and decisions about love, relationships, and sex. I met my boyfriend in college and married a few years later. Both of us were young and naive. As two young adults starting a relationship and entering a marriage, we barely knew much about ourselves and knew very little or nothing about each other. But we were married and over the coming weeks, months, and years we would encounter the truth and reality of life and the impact of our choices and decisions in getting married at that stage.

What I thought falling in love, been in relationship, getting married, and life would be and how things turned out and what I experienced were so far from what I had imagined. I wanted to feel and experience deep love, passion, romance, intimacy, and personal and spiritual growth. But the focus of our relationship immediately changed. All our energy, time, and resources were directed to getting married and how to make that public showcase of the wedding perfect. The emphasis of our love and relationship shifted to the wedding instead of cultivating love and happiness. There was no thought or plan put into the days and years that will follow after the music of the wedding bells were over. Love and marriage—which one comes first? Did I know what I was doing or getting myself into? Did he know what he was doing and getting himself into? It took me years to get a full understanding of the answers to those questions.

Why Did I Get Married?

I knew from a very early age that love is an important aspect of my essence. I knew this even though I never saw love expressed and demonstrated in a deep and meaningful way around me. I just had the knowingness that it exists and it's something I wanted to experience. So why did I get married? Was it to share and experience the love I knew existed? I had love in my heart and wanted to experience and share it. I wanted to love and be loved. As I reflected back on my decision to get married at such an early age, I realized that it was more a choice to leave home, to move out, and to escape the rigid and overly strict way of life in my family. There was a big disconnection between what I was expected to be, what was expected of me, and what I wanted and expected for myself. I wanted to be happy and free from my sheltered upbringing. My desire was to move out and away from the restrictive and punitive rules of my family and to live life without fear of what my parents would do or think of me. I wanted to be happy. I wanted the freedom to love and be loved. I wanted to feel alive. I needed to leave home. My parents would never let me move out on my own. How else could I leave home and still have a respectful relationship with my parents and all my other siblings? How could I leave home without them disowning me or without them feeling shamed or disgraced by my actions?

This was my ticket to freedom and happiness. This was my ticket to my own life—to live in Loveland and happiness. Why? Because I wanted to leave home yesterday, and being in a relationship for the purpose of getting married was the only way my parents would ever endorse my decision to move out and to do so with their blessing. Two things became my obsessional desires: find love and get married. I did and it fulfilled its intended purpose.

Is marriage the only way to have and experience personal and intimate love? I wanted love, happiness, and the freedom to live life without the tyrannical grip of my parents. So I got married so young and did exactly what I was programmed to believe in and what I thought was important to my life at that time.

The Rewards and Consequences of Hasty Love and Life Decisions

Looking back at those decisions I made some twenty five years ago, I feel proud and blessed with the gifts of our four sons, three biological and one adopted. But I am also filled with many regrets. I don't regret falling in love and getting married, but I do regret what it turned out to be. I let myself stay in a relationship in which I was unhappy and miserable for years. I did what I thought would give me what I wanted, but I never experienced the love nor lived the happy life I desired. I had spent that most important phase of my life living someone else's life. I have been unhappy, empty, and dying inside for years. I survived by suppressing which turned into anger, frustration, and eventually resentment towards my husband. So I started asking myself why I stayed even when I knew from the beginning that my most important needs were not being met? What went wrong? What is my life about? What should I tell my children about what love is and what life is about? Should I tell my family and friends that I am not happy and haven't been happy in years? What would they think of me? Would they understand? Would they blame me? The only person I need to tell the truth to and be honest with is myself first, and I did. Once you know the truth, live it. The truth shall set you free. This freed me and gave me clarity.

What do I really deserve? What do I now value most in life and what matters to me today and for the remainder of the life I have left? How can I be a better role model for my children and those around me? How can I use my experiences and learning to live a more fulfilled life and help my children live better lives and not make the same mistakes? What can I learn from my experiences which will help me to grow and become a better person because of it?

The Most Important Lesson I Learned from My Past

As I reflect on the past, I ask myself what's the most important lesson I learned and what would I do differently today before getting into any relationship?

The most important thing I learned from my past experiences is to first create and have a better relationship with myself. I now know where my mistakes came from. I wanted to be in love and for someone to love me, but like almost everyone, no one taught me I needed to love myself first. The second mistake I made was in my selection. These two mistakes were out of ignorance.

Don't do what I did back then if you haven't already. I strongly suggest before you begin seeking an intimate relationship to develop a deep connection with and love for yourself.

2

The Most Important Relationship — The Relationship with Yourself

The Importance of Self-Love

Your relationship with yourself is the **blueprint** that determines all other relationships in your life. This is why it is the most important relationship in your life. It is the model from which every other relationship in your life is shaped. It sets the standards, the depth of the love you are willing to give, as well as the rules of how to relate with others and how others should relate with you. Keep in mind that it is the quality of the relationship you have with yourself that defines the quality of your relationship with others.

You must have heard phrases such as "You have to love yourself before you can love anyone else" or "You have to love yourself before anyone can love you." These statements point to a core universal belief that when we love ourselves we create the foundation for loving others, and we create the space in our heart for having meaningful relationships with others. And to love yourself is to know yourself. It is when you love yourself, value yourself, cherish yourself, honour and respect yourself that you will have a strong and authentic relationship with others. And it is when you love yourself, value yourself, and respect who you are that you open to authentically love, accept, and be okay with who and what others choose to be. You will love them as you love yourself, you will value them as you value yourself, you will cherish them as you cherish yourself, and you will treat them as you treat yourself. This is why your relationship with yourself is often described in Neuro-Linguistic Programming (NLP) terms as "the working model" against which all your other relationships are referenced and patterned.

Why is it important to love, value, accept, and know ourselves? Because it is when you love and value yourself that you know your worthiness as well as know who you are. And you can make conscious and intelligent choices about who to get into a relationship with so he or she will complement and magnify who you already are and what you already have.

You cannot give to anyone that which you do not have. Getting into a relationship and expecting the other person to fill what it is you believe is lacking and missing within you, whether it's love or happiness, self-esteem or worthiness, is the root of a lot of relationship and marriage breakdowns. Think about it, how can you have and share a great relationship with someone when the most important relationship in your life is toxic or doesn't even exist? What will you bring into and give to a relationship? You can't give what you have not given to yourself or what you don't have.

Franca: When I got married at twenty-two, I brought into the marriage unhealthy patterns like anger, frustration, and hurt. Why? Because I never took the time to evaluate my life, I had no sense of direction other than walking down the aisle, and I inherited my parents' beliefs and values. I didn't understand why I clashed with their rigid way of thinking. I realize now that I had built barriers of the unhealthy references that I had about relationships, all of which I have built in order to protect myself from getting hurt and as a way to control the relationship I was in. As a result, I settled for partners that provided me with certainty and safety, instead of love, fun, and adventure which is my true essence.

Stop for a moment and ask yourself, what barriers have you built around love? What old stories are you holding onto? Are you ready to forgive and let go? Are you ready to move forward happily and honestly?

The Walls of Fear

The walls you build to protect yourself from fear and the possible pain of love are the same walls blocking you from getting and experiencing the love and the relationship you want and deserve. When you do this you become the prisoner in the prison of your fear of love and pain.

For you to break through, move forward, and be in a relationship where love flows freely and abundantly, it's important that you understand the root of fears and the negative association you may have unknowingly made regarding love and relationships, and then release their anchors.

The Courage to Give up Fear and Embrace Love

Rhonda, the older of two girls, grew up with a father who was a controlling and jealous tyrant who decided the best way to keep their mother "at point" was to abuse her verbally, emotionally, and physically. There was a day he beat her so unbearably that she was hospitalized for days. He then extended his territorial control machine to Rhonda. No one was left out. When Rhonda was twelve, he intensified his anger towards her and on one occasion, he decided to put his hands around her neck and strangle her to death once and for all. Fortunately, her sister was home witnessing her father attempting to end Rhonda's life. She screamed, cried, and begged, "Please, Daddy, quit killing Rhonda" until he stopped and released the chokehold leaving Rhonda gasping for air.

Rhonda began asking the tough questions: "What is wrong with my father? What's wrong with my mother? Why didn't my mother leave?" She finally did. It took her two years to summon her inner strength to tell herself the truth that enough is enough and tell him that she's done with him and the marriage. She got him to pack and move out.

He showed up on Father's Day but not to go out for brunch with the family as they had planned; he had other plans in mind. It was a perfect day to carry out his final act to prove his masculinity and superiority, and set the record straight once and for all that he is a powerful man and should never be disrespected or humiliated. After her mother closed the house door and started walking toward her car that was parked in the driveway, her father, who pretended he needed his jacket from the trunk of his car, watched her carefully and calmly. He opened the trunk and instead of taking out his jacket, he picked up a loaded rifle. Just as she turned toward him, he pointed the gun at her and yelled out, "You made me do this!" He shot her in the stomach and she doubled over. He then turned and aimed the gun at Rhonda. Her tender heart sank. She thought she was next, but he pointed it again at his wife and shot her one more time. She dropped to the ground. The last bullet went through her hitting the car horn as well. Neighbours watched with panic. Everyone was dialing 911.

As if the drama and terror weren't enough, he started walking towards Rhonda. Just a few feet from her, he stopped then bent to his knees and pointed the rifle at his temple. Rhonda screamed, "No, Dad! Please stop! No!" He fired it, killing himself. Rhonda was terror stricken and frozen on the spot. Within minutes police cars and sirens filled the entire street. The neighbours were in complete disbelief. The unthinkable had happened. A father had killed his wife and the mother of his children, and then killed himself. The two teenage girls were left with the worst of trauma of love, marriage, and life. This is a classic tale of love gone wrong.

To find solace, Rhonda called her boyfriend and begged him to come over. When he and his father arrived, they were shocked at the extent of what had happened. Her boyfriend and his father didn't know how to handle or respond to the situation and didn't know how to comfort or care for Rhonda. It was beyond what they could process. "It's not our place to be here," the father said softly to the son, and they left. They left Rhonda alone, unknowingly reinforcing her fear and belief that no one would ever want to be with her again. From that point on, she feared she would always be alone. She was branded as "the girl who had watched her parents die."

The terror and trauma Rhonda experienced witnessing the murderous and suicidal end of her parents' lives left her with the profound fear and belief that she didn't deserve to be alive. She was convinced that she was "a loser" and was "not good enough," just like her father had told her many times. The pain and grief of the loss of her parents drove Rhonda to do whatever she could to numb the pain and fear: drink too much, work crazy hours, and spend too much.

The fear and hopelessness took over her mental and emotional power to the point that she wanted to take her own life three times.

For years she suffered and underwent all kinds of therapies, grief groups, read hundreds of books, and attended self-help seminars to come to terms with her parents' deaths. Although nothing she tried worked, she uncovered the truth which led to a breakthrough. She became aware that "fear was at the root of my troubles. Not the memories of the murder/suicide, not the years of feeling guilty and worthless, not the overworking, drinking, and spending spree I indulged in to numb my pain. Those were only symptoms of the unconscious fear that was running my life. Although I had tried to change these destructive behaviours through willpower, it had never worked because the core of my problem was the primal fear that I was a loser, I was not good enough."

With the conscious realization of the root cause of her personal, emotional, behavioural, and relationship challenges, she confronted her limiting beliefs, let go of the magnetic pull of fear and embraced love. "You don't have to earn or deserve love. You are love. Love is never about how others treat you. It's always about how you are treating yourself, and how you are sharing that overflow with others," Rhonda wrote.

Your essence is love. You have remarkable power to attract the love, a relationship, and your beloved to manifest into your life. This power is the power of love you have within you.

–Franca Navarra

Chapter

3

Selection
The Most Important Relationship Decision

What's the single most important decision in a relationship? What is it that defines and determines the quality and destiny of any relationship? What is it that differentiates a long-lasting, extraordinary, passionate, loving, and fulfilling relationship from one that's boring, miserable, broken, and eventually ends in a separation?

The most important decision in the creation of any relationship is selection. You see, it is who you select to get into a relationship with that determines the quality, longevity, and destiny of your relationship. It is the moment of your decision as to whom you choose to be in relationship with that sets the standards, tone, quality, and future of your relationship in motion. Remember that it is the person with whom you choose to enter into a relationship that produces the level and depth of love, happiness, and fulfillment or the level of emptiness and pain the two of you will experience in the relationship.

Human relationship is the most significant vehicle in which we experience the deepest love and ecstasy, as well as the deepest heartbreak and sorrow. Keep this in mind: **the purpose of a relationship is to share human experiences and intensify human emotions.** This is why who you choose to be in a relationship with is the most decisive factor in ensuring the amount of joy and playfulness or the misery and emptiness you will feel and experience in your relationship. And this is the reason selection is what sets the foundation of what and how your relationship will be. If you didn't know this before, know it now; whether it's a long-term relationship, a marriage, a vacation fling, or a one-night stand, **the person you select to be in a relationship with is the catalytic force that determines the quality and intensity of the love, passion, satisfaction, or boredom and misery you will experience.**

According to Human Needs Psychology (HNP), 90% of the success or failure of any relationship is significantly based on the person you choose to be in relationship with. The lasting success or early breakup of any relationship can be traced to the moment the selection of the person to be in a relationship with was made. Who you select to get into a relationship with will powerfully affect the quality of your relationship, the quality of your love, the quality of your happiness, the quality of your health, and your overall quality of your life, for better or worse. When you **intelligently make** the **right selection**, the **rewards** in your relationship and your life are extraordinary. When you **foolishly** make the **wrong selection** the **consequences** are **fatal** to every aspect of your life.

66 *The quality of your relationship is the quality of your selection.* 99

–Lucas Asu

Most people believe that human beings are very complex creatures and are challenging to understand. This may be true when a person has limited knowledge and understanding of people and human nature. What you are learning from this book will massively enhance your understanding of your fellow human beings. When you make an intelligent selection you can have extraordinary and lasting relationships.

The Starting Point of Selection

Step 1: Know Yourself

Where do you begin to look for that perfect partner? The first guideline to help you select the right relationship partner mandates that you know yourself. It's by knowing who you are at your core that you will know what kind and type of person you want to attract and have a relationship with. If you don't know who you are and what you value in a relationship, it will be challenging for you to select the right person. So knowing yourself helps you define with more clarity what exactly you want in a relationship and who you want to be in a relationship with. It's that deep understanding of yourself that can inspire you to select the right relationship with clarity and certainty.

If you are a woman who is more tuned into her feminine energy, you will be more attracted to a man with strong masculine energy. If you are a woman who has a stronger masculine side, you will be drawn to your polar match: a man who has a more nurturing nature. If you are a woman with a balanced nature, you will be drawn to a man whose energy is also in balance. The same dynamics are true for men.

2: Suitable Synergy

Sexual passion requires a masculine core and a vibrant feminine essence. When two people's energies are identical then there will be a neutralized sexual alliance. This type of relationship could have love but no passion and this is the primary cause of a low sexual flame in relationships. Keep in mind that we all have these energy systems within us and we all have the capabilities to switch. Each of us has a core where we live predominantly. You are always drawn and attracted to someone who is in synergy with your core.

3: Your Nature

Is your nature masculine, feminine, or balanced? In one of the best relationship books we read while doing research for this book, *The Way of the Superior Man* by David Deida, it is reported that 80% of all relationships are made up of a man with a more masculine essence and a woman with a more feminine essence, and only about 10% of couples have a balanced or neutral sexual essence. The other 10% of couples are made up of a more feminine man and a more masculine woman. What's your core? Are you more masculine or more feminine or are you balanced in your energy?

How Your Emotions Impact Your Relationship Choices

Emotions are the filters that control our decision-making process. As human beings we are able to feel and experience an unlimited array of emotions. We can feel these emotions in our bodies, in our hearts, and deep in our core. The emotions you live with have a powerful influence on who you select to be in a relationship with. People who live with negative emotions such as fear or anxiety, anger or depression, often unknowingly shut down their conscious and logical thinking processes and make poor and desperate choices not based on what they truly want and deserve, but based on the broken feelings they are trying to run away from. These emotions become a reflection of their choices as well as what they carry into their relationship. Your relationship will then become a reflection of these emotions and you are going to behave consistently with how you feel. But if you live in emotional states such as love, happiness, fun, and appreciation then your selection will also be a reflection of your dominant emotional states since you will be more conscious of the quality of your choice. Your selection will reflect your standards. Let me remind you again that **a relationship is a place we go to share and intensify our experiences and emotions**. What you bring into the relationship is what you are going to be sharing and that's what will be magnified. Make sure before and during your selection or dating period you are living in emotional states that make you feel confident and whole. This is when you can make your selection decision with clarity, intention, and certainty based on what you truly want and deserve and bring the best of yourself into the relationship.

By knowing yourself, you are selecting what and who you are going to be and what you bring and contribute to your relationship. Your relationship will be a reflection of who you are, because who you are is what will show up and what will be shared and therefore intensified.

Chapter

4

Who Do You Want to Become?

As you may already know, our intention is to share with you insights, tools, and strategies to help you create and have an extraordinary, loving, passionate, and fulfilling relationship. To do that, you have to go beyond. As much as it is important to know who you are, it is even more important to decide who you want to become. Why is this important? **You don't attract what you want, you attract what you are.** We know you may be saying to yourself now "I like who I am, so why do you want me to become someone else?" There's always room for growth and improvement in anyone's life. No matter how much you love and like yourself, you can always become better and more as a person. So don't be defensive about this. You wouldn't be reading this book unless you were already open-minded, open to suggestions, or someone who is driven by growth and is coachable. So evaluate who you have let yourself be and decide now who you want to become today, not who you were in your past. Who do you want to become mentally, emotionally, psychologically and spiritually? What new personality and character traits will you embody?

Remember that it is the person you become who is going to greatly determine who you attract into your life and the kind and quality of relationship you are going to have. Allow yourself to go deeper and bring out the best that's within you. When you do, you will attract the qualities of who you are in the person you select to be in a relationship with. Like attracts like. Who will you attract into your life and what will the quality of your relationship be when you show up as the best of you every day? By deciding what you are going to become, you are also deciding what you are going to attract and what you want your relationship to be like.

Know What You Want

There is a principle in life that in order to get what you want, you must first know what it is you want. How can you get what you want when you don't know what it is? Do you want sex, a casual relationship, a common-law partner, or the traditional institution of marriage? Knowing what you want helps you seek a partner that has reciprocal desires. One of the core principles of the Law of Attraction is "like attracts like." If you want a casual relationship for sexual intentions, you will not be a perfect fit for someone who wants to get into a relationship for the purpose of growing it into a marriage and starting a family. Having clarity and knowing what you want prevents confusion of intention during your selection or dating period. This is how you get what you want by knowing and being honest about what it is that will give you the greatest level of love, passion, and fulfillment. To get what you want you must know what you desire and deserve.

*What qualities and character traits do you want the person you want to be in relationship with to have?

*What values and beliefs do you value most and want that person to also already have?

*What are some of the things you want to have in common with this person you intend to be in a relationship with?

*What's your relationship vision? Describe your relationship vision in detail. Be clear and specific.

Be Smart. Be Wise.

Why do they want to be in a relationship? Are they internally motivated because they love you and because you share similar interests with them? Or are they externally induced by social significance to be in a relationship and are motivated because someone else wants them to be in a relationship with you?

Motive and Intention Matter

I will never forget the responses I received when I asked couples why they got married. One couple said, "Because our pastor said he saw a vision of us being in love and getting married." Another time, one man's wife declared, "We got married because my family kept telling me he is a nice man and nice men are hard to find these days." A young man in another relationship said he chose his partner because she was blonde and would give him beautiful babies. The challenge that couples face—and the eventual separations they go through—are due to poor decisions and wrong motives for engaging in a long-term committed relationship. This is because when these external pressures or externally induced motives are fulfilled there will be no more drive, energy, or purpose to be in the relationship. This means that one person's desire for love from his or her partner will diminish drastically and the passion that bonded them at the beginning immediately evaporates. No company hires anyone because that person just wants a job. A company hires someone who can do the job, will fit in with the culture of the environment, and will get along with others harmoniously to help accomplish the intended mission. Remember that the clearer you are about what you want in a relationship, the better you will be at attracting, meeting, and having that right person in your life. You deserve a loving, passionate, and fulfilling relationship. And you can have it when you choose your relationship partner wisely.

The Biggest Mistake Men and Women Make During Dating

People's nature rarely changes. Save yourself years, if not a lifetime, of regrets and misery by taking the time to select the person that meets what it is that you want and deserve in a relationship. The biggest mistake most men and women make during the selection process is that they meet and choose a partner that they know from the beginning does not have even half of what they are looking for but will convince themselves that they will be able to change or mold the person to fit into what they want. The belief that they will change to conform to what you want them to be is erroneous. This is the primary cause of unhappiness, misery, and fallouts that we see in most relationships and marriages today. It is your responsibility, and only you alone can fulfill this responsibility, to select the person that already has the values, beliefs, and the personality traits you seek in a relationship partner. Keep in mind that people's nature rarely changes. People have the right to be who they choose to be. Your task is to find and choose someone who already has all that you are looking for.

You don't have to have a PhD in mind reading in order to know more about someone and have a glimpse into their personality. In fact, most people crave to be known and can't help but reveal themselves. All you need is a little **curiosity** and **sensory acuity**.

1: Action, Not Words: Pay serious attention to what they do, not so much to what they say because in real life, action is more important than words. It is more so through their actions and behaviours than their words and intention that their character is revealed. Does she or he try to create more time and spend time with you or make excuses that certain things always come up that become a higher priority than you? If you are significantly important to them, then they will make communicating with you, seeing you, and spending time with you a priority, won't they?

2: Dominant Theme of Their Conversation: Listen actively to what his or her central conversation is about. Does she or he think and speak about you, the relationship, and your shared future plans or is her or his conversation centralized around his or her work, plans, business, money, and friends? What they speak most about reveals and says more about what they value most and care about in life.

3: Playing Hard to Get: We all love mysteries, don't we? Dating the lover who is "playing hard to get" can sometimes be so intriguing to the other person that they become spellbound and lose touch with reality. No matter how much you may be fascinated by this individual, the distancing of themselves from you could mean he or she is emotionally unavailable and is emotionally inaccessible for the deep, intimate love you want.

4: Emotional States: Does he or she have a full presence and a happy and cheerful disposition or an anxious and restless emotional state? A person's emotional state communicates unerringly what is preoccupying a person's mental focus and energy and what is happening in their lives. Their primary emotional states help you to know whether they are emotionally available, emotionally rich, and emotionally ready for a relationship or whether they are emotionally bankrupt seeking an emotional rescue mate or someone to dump their emotional garbage on.

Consequences of Selecting the Wrong Partner

The failure to select the right partner for your relationship has tremendous consequences. These consequences are the price people pay for their poor choices when selecting who to be with in a relationship or who to get married to. The lack of clarity from the onset in your selection process is what leads to these consequences, some of which are lack of fulfillment, loneliness, infidelity, emotional and physical abuse, excessive drinking, gambling, accumulation of debt, raising children alone even while you have a partner, and eventual separation or divorce. People have lost their health and sometimes their lives due to the poor selection of the person they choose to get into a relationship with or get married to. You can prevent all of these and much more when you take your time to select intelligently.

Some Suggestions on How to Select the Right Relationship Partner:

1: Don't settle. Have absolute clarity on what you want and the quality of a relationship you deserve.

2: Choose your relationship partner from a place of wholeness and worthiness.

3: Don't be desperate. Desperate people always end up with the wrong relationship. When you are desperate you always make the wrong choice. Let your decision for love be guided by your true desire for what you really want in a relationship. Believe that person you seek exists and you will meet each other.

4: You have the right to be in the right relationship and you deserve an extraordinary, loving, passionate, and fulfilling relationship.

5: You have one life to live. Don't waste it with the wrong person. Select wisely. Your happiness and fulfillment largely depend on it.

Chapter

5

The Six Needs of a Relationship

Everyone seeking a relationship or that is in a relationship believes at some level of their consciousness that if they could just find a Cupid's arrow, they would have the magic secret to their lover's heart. Then from that moment onward, their relationship will be filled with the deepest passion, love, and ecstasy forever.

You can't build a relationship based on fairytales. For you to have your dream relationship, for you to have an extraordinary quality relationship, you first need to consciously and intelligently select the right person, as you read in Chapter Two. Without that essential step, nothing you do can keep that relationship vibrant nor will it even last.

For your relationship to have that aliveness and for the love and passion to last beyond the euphoria of the first few dates, you need to understand the **Six Needs** of a relationship.

These **Six Needs** represent the most profound breakthrough in **Human Needs Psychology** (HNP) in regards to **relationships**. This leading-edge science now enables us to understand with more accuracy and precision the **intrinsic drives** that every woman and man strives to **fulfill** in a relationship and in their lives in order to feel **fully alive,** to have a **sense of meaning** about their lives, and to be **deeply fulfilled**.

Through cultural and social **evolutionary conditioning** men and women are unconsciously or consciously seeking a relationship, as it's been proven through time as the most **dependable vehicle** to meet their **Human Needs** at a **higher** and **deeper** level. After all, a relationship is a **place** we go to **meet our needs** through **sharing experiences** and **intensifying emotions**.

These Six Needs are not wishes, wants, or desires. They are **Human Needs** that must be met otherwise there will be no purpose for that person you are in a relationship with to be alive; their life will have no sense of meaning. These Needs are what make us feel alive. These Needs are what give us a sense of certainty, meaning, and fulfillment.

No one would choose to be in a relationship with you and no one would give you a chance for a first date if they knew you don't have what it takes and can't fulfill the needs they value the most in life and in a relationship. As you learn and understand what these needs are, and, with diligence and practice, you are able to meet them on a consistent basis at the highest intensity, you will have a relationship that's magical, exceptional, and one that a few will even envy and others will see as an inspiration.

These Needs are the golden secret keys to the hidden and mysterious castle of love that so many are searching for but only a handful have found. You are about to unravel that golden secret to having everlasting passion, love, and fulfillment in your relationships. In fact, life, love, and relationships will no longer be a mystery but an exciting adventure as you master these Six Needs and how to consistently fulfill them in your relationship. The drive to meet these Needs, as you have read, is the core unconscious reason people get into relationships.

Your primary task is to understand which of these Six Needs the person you are in a relationship with values the most. Then for you to honour and appreciate what they have been wired to value and then fulfill those needs. When you do they will feel alive, loved, and fulfilled. The failure to know and meet these Needs is the fundamental cause of emptiness, misery, anger, and even rage in a relationship.

These Six Needs are what all human beings, regardless of geography, culture, background, colour, religion, or gender, strive to meet every moment. And the place we have all been programmed to depend upon the most to fulfill these Needs is through relationships.

The first four Needs are the Fundamental or Survival Needs. You can meet all these four Needs and you will have a good life and some level of happiness, but you won't be fulfilled and have a sense of meaning in your life. To experience the deepest joy, fulfillment, and meaning, you must meet the last two Needs: your Spiritual Needs.

When you shift your focus from the Fundamental or Survival Needs to your Spiritual Needs, you will have a quality of relationship and life that will be unmatched. When you help your partner meet not only the first four Fundamental or Survival Needs but also the last two Spiritual Needs, both of you will experience a new level of depth of love and fulfillment in your relationship and in your lives.

#1: Certainty: The Drive to Feel Safe and Be Comfortable

Most people don't get into a relationship to experience love. Most people get into a relationship in order to enhance their sense of security and comfort first above all else. The Need for safety or security is one of the most essential Human Needs we all value. Without this Need, nothing else matters. This Need is the foundation and the mechanism that ensures we are first safe and protected and that we are at least comfortable and happy. The Need for Certainty or comfort is the first primary filter in everyone's relationship decision making process.

As you seek love and a relationship, it is important to ask yourself if you are the kind of person the person you want to be in a relationship with will feel safe, comfortable, and happy to share love with. Everyone values their life. Everyone wants to be comfortable and be loved. So for them to go out on a date with you, to get into a relationship with you, and to even consider marrying you, their unconscious filter will run that checklist first to make sure they will be safe, comfortable, happy, and loved. This is a worldwide behavioural pattern whether the person is in Toronto, Johannesburg, Beijing, Paris, or Rio de Janeiro. Remember these Needs are universal. It's only when this feeling of certainty is provided along with some guarantee that it will continuously be met, and that they will be safe, comfortable, happy, and loved that you'll get the green light for their love and for a relationship. Without certainty, your prospect for anyone's love will be shut down.

This is why building rapport and trust is so vital from the start, as everyone wants to be with someone they can be comfortable with and freely share who they are. You can have rapport within a few seconds of a conversation with someone, but the trust of love is something you earn through your behaviours and your actions, not just through words.

As we mentioned earlier, relationships and marriages throughout human history are means to enhance people's sense of security and comfort. People don't live on intentions and big promises. Human beings the world over have been and are striving for a better quality of life they can enjoy now while they plan for an even brighter future. What they seek is someone they have an attraction, a likeness, or love for that they can do that with.

You can have a quality short-term love and sexual exchange with anyone. But for those that want to create their dream relationship and make it extraordinary and long-lasting, first create the certainty within your personality and work on having the security, which is social and economic stability, in your own life. Without a base level certainty, you and your lover will have a lot of unnecessary pressure and stress and will deprive yourselves, and at some point your children, of some comfort and pleasures life has to offer.

Money cannot solve all the problems people face in their relationships and marriages, but it can eliminate a lot of the unnecessary economic stress and humiliation most couples experience. You have probably heard "we can't afford it," "we can't do that because we don't have the money for that," or "we can't go there because it's just too expensive and we have bills to pay."

If you are entering a new relationship, make sure the person you are selecting has and can meet your own criteria of what a safe, secure, comfortable, happy, and loving relationship constitutes.

How certain are you that they love you and they can contribute to your happiness?

How certain are you that they will continue to love you even more tomorrow and five years from now?

Are they economically driven to ensure both of you have a great quality of life that reflects your dreams and goals and the life you want to live?

What do they value when it comes to love, money, work, and family?

Franca: Throughout my marriage, even though we have been married for more than twenty years, I still asked questions such as "Do you still love me?" and "Do you still find me attractive?" These are all certainty-oriented questions. I needed the feeling of approval and reassurance to have that sense of certainty that I am still loved and I am still attractive. My husband had a different way of meeting his need for certainty. For him it was making sure we had enough to eat and pay our bills. This provided him with a great sense of security and stability.

Everyone has a different strategy for meeting their Need for certainty in a relationship. Some people need to hear "I love you" every day and sometimes many times in a day. They won't feel you love them without this while others just need an intimate touch or the knowledge that financially they have the means to live comfortably.

The value of certainty is that it gives stability to a relationship.

What we have discovered over the years through direct experiences of coaching couples and assisting them to improve the quality of their relationships is that when individuals become too comfortable in their relationships, boredom sets in. This is when the same certainty that was needed to create the relationship is now a neutralizing force in the relationship. This is a problem the second Human Need will solve.

Are You Caring or Carrying?

Is your relationship based on caring or carrying? Most people in relationships or marriages associate giving and showing love with taking on an enormous amount of the responsibilities in the relationship, including the things their lover can do for herself or himself. Taking on more than you can do is carrying, not caring.

What's driving this behaviour? What is driving this behaviour is the belief that "I can do it better, I can do it faster." This rationalization reinforces the belief that you must keep doing everything in order to maintain a sense of control. When this happens, your intention for loving and caring will be turned to "carrying" your loved ones.

Love, care, and support your lover and loved ones. But let go of your beliefs that only you can do it faster, quicker, and better. Caring is love, carrying is control. Most carriers are addicted to being in control. When you let go of this pattern you give those that you love and care about the space and the opportunity to develop and use their potential.

#2: The Need for Variety/Romantic Ecstasy

66 *Unless it's mad, passionate, extraordinary love then it's a waste of time. There are too many mediocre things in life and love should never be one of them.* 99

–Unknown

Human beings are pattern-driven creatures. When we do something and it works, we most often just want to do it over and

39

over again. This may be effective and efficient at your work or business, but not in a relationship. In life and in relationships, human beings love surprises and anything that excites and stimulates them.

Certainty means: I love you and I will always love you. My love for you is assured and guaranteed.

Variety means: Kiss me passionately. Touch me with the fire of your soul like never before.

How fun is your relationship? Do you and your lover do different things regularly or do you not even remember the last time the two of you went for a walk together or had a date night and did something out of the ordinary?

Without romantic ecstasy the love in your relationship will eventually die no matter how much security and stability you provide. Romantic ecstasy is the fire that keeps your love vibrant, passionate, and intense and your attraction for each other deep.

If the two of you do the same things and go to the same places and make love the same way, then your relationship is chronically suffering and lacking romantic ecstasy. It's time to rekindle passion, playfulness, and spontaneity in your relationship. This is what Romantic Ecstasy can bring into your relationship and your life.

Franca: I remember when my husband was my boyfriend we made scheduling our dates a priority. We were silly, playful, went places and did different things. It was always fun when we were together. There was this moment we were kissing very passionately in the car in the mall parking lot and someone that was passing by stopped and said, "You guys need a room." Back then, in spite of our strict parents and strict religious upbringing, we always found ways to see each other, and the time we spent together was beautiful.

But when we got married, life became super busy and go, go, go. Our focus and energies drastically shifted from making our relationship and each other a priority to making work, paying bills, keeping the house in order, and starting a family our total focus. We forgot and lost what brought us together in the first place. We got too certain, too comfortable, and took each other's love and our relationship for granted. We lost the sense of what love is. Life became mundane. We barely laughed, barely kissed, barely touched each other, and "I love you" became just like "good morning." We made everything and everyone a priority over keeping our love and relationship vibrant and alive.

What Happens to the Relationship When it Becomes Too Predictable?

Without amusement, fun, and excitement in a relationship, boredom will creep in and destroy your attraction for each other and even your relationship. One of the primary causes of relationship failure is boredom. Boredom is the most destructive relationship pattern and unintentionally kills the love and passion in a relationship. Most relationships end not because of lack of love but because the lack the magic of passion, playfulness, laughter, and spontaneous romance.

To keep a relationship vibrant and alive, couples must make fulfilling each other's Need for Romantic Ecstasy as important as providing the certainty and the stability for their relationship.

The most common problem that keeps coming up over and over from the married couples we coach is that the women complain that their husbands have become so boring and as a result, they (the wives) have lost connection and sexual attraction to them. Do you know that one of the consequences of a boring relationship is cheating? Yes! You read that right, cheating. Infidelity is the price most couples pay for boredom they created and allowed to infest their relationships. In up to fifty percent of these marriages we mentioned, the women have cheated on their "boring" husbands, and most of these women are planning their separation. Before you turn on your filters of righteousness and before you pass your judgment and sentence these women, let's remind you again that these Needs are not wishes, desires, or wants; they are Needs that must be met at all costs.

When you are passionate, boredom disappears and magic appears.

No matter how much money you make in your job or business, no matter how much you love your children, and no matter how organized your house is, if you don't make time for romantic ecstasy with your love, you will lose her or him. You may not lose them physically, but you may lose your lover emotionally.

Romantic ecstasy requires creativity, spontaneity, and thoughtfulness. Love with romantic ecstasy makes being in love an extraordinary and magical experience. Create your romantic magic.

What are the simple things you can spontaneously do that will totally surprise and light up your lover? Can you write something beautiful on the mirror for them or a note on a piece of paper and sneak it in her purse or in his wallet?

#3: *The Need to Feel Special and Important*

You can create and have an extraordinary quality of relationship when you have extraordinary insights and skills for such a relationship.

One of the most powerful ways to deepen your connection and intensify the love and passion in your relationship with your lover is to create a relationship environment in which your lover feels emotionally secure and so special with you and in your world.

Women flourish through compliments and praise and men thrive with respect. Both women and men are genetically programmed with the same Need to feel important. This Need for women is to feel special and for men it is to feel significant. Both have the same Need to feel important. Well, at least Franca and I do.

Men: At all times your lady needs to feel that she's special and she is the most important person in your world. That's right, she needs to feel and know she's the number one person in your life all the time. This should be done not just in private but also in public, and, most especially, at a social gathering or party when other women are around. Anything other than your lady feeling special and important could trigger doubts and feelings of uncertainty in her inner world about her place in your life. Your lady will blossom and be radiant like a well-tended summer garden when you feed her with compliments about her external beauty and inner qualities or personality. It should be done from an honest and loving place because you are driven by your deep love for her. Complimenting and praising your lady is an act of love; it's a demonstration of what she truly means to you and how much she matters in your life.

Praise the way she makes love to you and how she makes you feel. Whatever you praise in your lady, she will develop and grow more into that quality. So when you compliment and praise your lady, you are not just causing her to feel that way but you are contributing to inspiring and calling forth more of that quality into her personality. This is the power of this strategy.

A word of caution: Always love your mother (if she's still alive), but no matter how close you are to her, always let your lady know she's the most important woman now in your life. Never create a situation in which your lady and your mother, or your lady and your female friend(s), have to compete to be more special to you than the other. Your mother is your mother. Always, always love her. Your female friends must also know both when you are with them and when your lady is present that now your lady is your queen. Any mixed messages (verbal or nonverbal) will put your trust, faithfulness, and loyalty into question. An extraordinary quality of relationship demands a high level of unquestionable trust and high standards.

Women: Make your man feel significant whenever he sets and achieves a goal, does something out of the ordinary for you or the children, takes initiative for something, or does a repair you have wanted done at home. Let him know how much you respect him for all that he does for you (and your children, if you have any). Let your man know he's the best and you are so happy that he's your man. A man will do anything just to know he is the best.

When a woman is not complimented and a man is not made to feel significant (both are not made to feel important), their life's energy will be weakened. A lot of women, including myself (Franca), do slide into depression and anxiety when we are not made to feel special or not made to feel that we are everything to the man we are in love with and giving our love to.

When your woman is made to feel she's special and important and when your man is made to feel he is respected, you will have a lasting, loving, and passionate extraordinary quality relationship.

Both women and men dish out abundant compliments and praise to each other during the early phases when they are proving themselves as worthy of each other's love and commitment. But it seems after they have successfully secured what they want and have settled warmly into the relationship, they become comfortable and stop complimenting and praising each other. They stop making each other important. Their work, the home, or the children becomes their most important priority. Why would intelligent loving people stop what was causing their love flames to burn strong, high, and hot? It's time you return to the simple habits that brought the two of you together and created your relationship. It's time to do what Tony Robbins recommends: "Do what you did at the beginning of your relationship and there won't be an end."

When was the last time you did something for your partner to make them feel they are special and needed? And what did your partner do for you that had you feeling special?

#4: The Need for Connection/Love

66 *My bounty is as endless as the sea, my love is deep; the more I give to thee the more I have, for both are infinite.* 99

–Romeo & Juliet, Shakespeare

What is it that we long for the most? What's that one thing that women and men would do anything for and would even fly from one end of the planet to the other for? It is the drive to meet this fourth **Need**, the **Need** for **Connection/Love**! This is a **Need** that we all need.

Everyone needs to feel loved. The need for love is at the core of our existence. But most people think love is too scary so they only allow themselves to settle for a basic connection. This is not love. This is just the desire to have companionship to overcome a hidden fear of being alone. Companionship will never give you the love, ecstasy, and fulfillment you deserve. Without deep quality of love your soul, your mind, your heart, and your essence are deprived of life's ultimate nourishment to feel fully alive and actualize your life's purpose.

It is through meeting this Need for love that we feel and experience the greatest joy, the highest high, and the most profound state of ecstasy. Love is considered one of the most powerful and penetrating emotions in human beings. I heard it said a long time ago that "the secret to eternal bliss is to love deeply."

The Need for Love is that magnetic force that draws men and women to do some of the craziest things. Women and men have climbed to the roof, climbed to a window, and jumped high-security fences in order to get to that special someone to experience the magic of a kiss, a touch, or that wild or quiet sexual moment to fulfill this Need for Love. It is what makes people get into relationships as temporary as a quickie in a parking lot, or nightclub washroom, or a one-night stand at a motel, and as short-term as in friends with benefits, and as long-term as marriage (although some marriages are temporary and short-term) in order for them to meet this most craved Need.

If love is such an important **Need** in our lives, one that both women and men cannot live without, why then are so many afraid of it? To answer this question, let's address the two primary fears human beings have in regards to love and relationships.

1: I am not enough. This is the primary fear that is stopping people from opening themselves up and allowing themselves to be loved and to give love. This fear stems from a person believing that there is something within that's missing or incomplete which means if they get into a relationship, they will not be able to live up to the expectations.

I am not beautiful enough, tall enough, my ass is not big enough, my breasts are not firm enough, my body is not toned enough, my teeth are not white enough, my skin is too dark, my skin is too white, my legs are too skinny, I don't know how to kiss, I am not good at giving blow jobs, I am not good in bed like those other girls, my penis is too short, I don't make enough money, I can't dance.

2: I won't be loved. Your unconscious reason for believing you are not enough is because you feel you won't be loved.

Follow the Persian poet Rūmī's advice and dismantle those invisible walls you have erected between you and the love you Need and deserve.

66 *Your task is not to seek for love, but to merely seek and find all the barriers within yourself that you have built against it.* 99

– *Rūmī*

Love is your gift.

Love is the foundation on which your relationship is built. The stronger the love, the stronger the relationship will be. The mistake some couples make is they spend their time trying fix the relationship or marriage instead of deepening the connection and love. It's love that's going to keep your relationship strong and lasting. Love is a Need, not a wish, desire, or want; it's a Need that must be met.

The moment you stop feeling and experiencing love you start losing your sense of aliveness.

Think of a baby. Experts have been ringing the alarm bells that without love and connection and touch or tactile stimulation, especially from the mother and/or the people around the baby, the baby will be love starved and will begin to shrink mentally, emotionally, and psychologically. Hence, permanent damage is done to this precious being's health and behaviour. Medical literature also proves that hospitalized patients that have people who love them, family and friends who visit and show love and caring, recover faster. Their survival rate even in terminal illnesses is higher. This is the power of Love. This is the power of this Need. Research now also shines light on the fact that in a workplace where the workers are engaged by management and colleagues (that are receiving connection and love), they tend to enjoy their work, perform better, and have higher productivity than those that are ignored. Pretty amazing, isn't it?

If love can help in speeding up the healing of the sick and help workers enjoy their work, perform better, and produce more results, imagine what it could do for you, for your relationship with your lover, and the people around you (especially children).

Most people are not succeeding because they believe "I am not enough" and they are not loved.

What happens when you stop giving and showing love to your lover?

Case Study:

Michelle and Steve have been married for over forty years and have three children in their twenties. Steve lives for his work and his life is prioritized around his work. He works seven days a week from 9 a.m. to 7 p.m. He rarely takes a holiday, and even when he does, it's with a miserable attitude. At work Steve is the happiest human being you'll ever meet, but at home he is always tired, withdrawn, and grumpy.

Michelle also works but she works only from Monday through Friday from 9 a.m. 'til 4 p.m. Michelle has gotten used to having dinner with their children, although she saves her dessert so she can spend time with Steve at the dinner table whenever he returns home from work.

The communication between Steve and Michelle is usually short. Their connection has diminished drastically and the love and passion is nearly nonexistent. They've become like roommates. Something is seriously missing. Michelle has been asking herself "Why did I get married? What happened? Is this all there is?" She is starving for a meaningful connection and a passionate and fulfilling love like they once had. "We had it before. We had it when we met. I was so happy and he was a happy man," Michelle said. "But everything changed about two years into the marriage when Steve took a job with this company even before we had any children. He is married to his job. He only comes home to eat and sleep. I have become some kind of mate and personal assistant; I care for the children, run errands, pay the bills, look after the house, and cook and clean. We don't touch each other anymore. I don't even remember the last time he kissed me, said something sweet, or made love to me. These things have become like Christmas. It makes me so sad every time I think this is what my life has come to be. I feel so sad. I don't like this."

Love is a Need we need in order to feel fully alive. Michelle is missing connection, love, and passion. The quality of relationship she once had and experienced had disappeared. Her husband's focus and energy are consumed by his job. He gets all his connection, love, and fulfillment from his job and his job relationships while the marriage is Michelle's primary source for meeting this important Need. And since this Need has not been met at a deeper level for years now, she is empty. She is suffering from starvation. She is not starving for food but for a deep connection, love, romance, intimacy, and meaningful conversation.

Over the years, this starvation, this emptiness, this loneliness (although she is married), has taken a toll on her happiness and has caused severe health problems. She's now on three medications for depression and low blood pressure.

Love is one of the fundamental Human Needs. This Need must be met or we lose that sense of aliveness. When this Need is not met for a prolonged period, the consequences are disastrous. When this Need is met in a deeper, meaningful, and fulfilling way, then life will become an enchanting experience. You deserve to have an extraordinary quality of love and relationship.

Need #5: The Need for Continuous Growth and Progress

Growth is the first of the two Spiritual Needs. Growth is also a natural law of life. There is no better area for continuous growth in someone's life than in their relationship. When a relationship isn't growing, it won't stay the same; it starts to break down. Growth creates progress and progress creates happiness. Growth is the seed of abundance. It's when your relationship with your lover is growing that you both develop abundance within yourselves and the capacity to give to each other limitlessly, and thereby experience a deeper level of love and fulfillment.

How can you be certain that your relationship is always growing and will always be growing? The best way for your relationship to be constantly improving in its quality is for you and your lover to be improving and growing yourselves. Your relationship will always reflect the level of your and your lover's personal growth. What this means to you is that the more you invest time and energy in improving and making yourselves better, the better your relationship becomes. And what this really means to you is that you and your lover will experience a depth and quality of connection, love, passion, and fulfillment beyond what you've ever believed could be possible. Why is this so? You see, the more you grow, the more you become, and the more you become, the more you have and can give to your beloved and your relationship. The ultimate secret to having your dream relationship is for you and your lover to become extraordinary in your personal development. It is through this that you become abundant and have an abundant capacity for love and all other things to have that extraordinary quality of relationship that is a reflection of your unified vision.

Franca: I know through my own experience that the connection and love my husband and I shared began to dissipate. Our marriage stopped growing. This was due to the lack of focus in nourishing each other with the essential Needs which we needed for our spirits to thrive. We both were caught up with everything else such as the house, the children, work, finances, family, and family events.

We never thought of investing in our personal development and growth. We didn't give to ourselves, we did not grow ourselves, and as a consequence we didn't have much to give to each other or to put into and grow the relationship. We stopped making progress in every aspect of ourselves. Our love and relationship had been running on an empty tank for a long time.

You must develop, expand, and grow yourselves so that you have much more to bring to each other and into the relationship. As you improve yourselves, you will develop better and more ways to meet each other's needs and grow a stronger relationship. In the process, both of you will experience the fulfillment that comes from having such a quality relationship. Growth nourishes and flourishes your relationship.

You cannot give what you don't have. To have all that you desire and to give all that you are capable of, grow. The purpose of growth is so you develop and have abundance. To grow your relationship, grow yourself. To make your relationship better, make yourself better. To have and enjoy that extraordinary quality of relationship and to make it lasting, you and your love must consistently be growing and refining yourselves and your strategies for fulfilling each other's Needs in a way that's consistent, enriching, and fulfilling. The more you grow yourself, the more abundance you have to give your lover and those you love and care about.

> *Growth creates abundance. The secret to having and experiencing abundance of love is growth.*

–Lucas Asu

Need #6: The Need for Contribution

Contribution is the last of the two Spiritual Needs. The purpose of growth, as you learned earlier, is so you can develop, become, and have an abundant capacity to love and for all the other riches of life. When love or a relationship is based on obligation, it lacks authenticity and dignity. Love and contribution should always come from a place of abundance and caring. You give because you have, love, and care.

Contribution in your relationship means you love passionately, and it is this love that inspires you every day to care so deeply that your nature is about loving and giving abundantly to your lover. For you, your life is about loving, growing, and contributing. This is what lights you up and what fills you up.

The first act of the expression of your love and contribution is measured in the depth and intensity of your love, passion, and caring for your lover and those around you. Your core purpose is to love your lover, and one of your missions on this planet is to love and worship him or her through love, and to contribute to your relationship with everything in you to make it extraordinary—one that others would be inspired to model. The love you have for your lover is pure, deep, and remarkably profound. In this type of relationship, no one is competing for the spotlight or control, and neither do they need approval from the outside world. Your nature is a loving contributor. You love loving and giving to your lover abundantly, and you do so without any ego because you just love with all your heart. You take total responsibility for how your lover feels because you consider your lover not separated from you. Your lover is you and you are your lover. Through the deep love you have for each other, you are one soul. Your unified and bigger vision and purpose is now to serve the world with the abundance of your love and all the blessings life has bestowed upon the two of you.

This brings us to the second mandate of your relationship—love and contribution. This is where you and your lover have grown and developed capacities beyond just fulfilling your own Needs. The calling of your relationship is contributing, serving, and giving to something or a cause that goes beyond you and your lover. This contribution means giving of yourselves, giving of your love, your presence, your time, your energy, your talent or skills, as well as your spiritual and material gifts. The purpose of your relationship now extends beyond the two of you. Life has given to you abundantly. Now it's time for you and your relationship to give back to life. This means the evolved purpose of your relationship is to inspire and impact others to awaken the extraordinary power of love that lies deep within them to ignite growth so they too can create their own magnificence.

Recently, we watched a TED Talk that reflects an outstanding and extraordinary relationship that is now contributing, inspiring, and transforming lives all over the world; it is the relationship, story, and philanthropic mission of Bill Gates and his wife, Melinda.

Franca and I were more than impressed with how one of the world's richest couples talked openly, candidly, and lovingly about their relationship, the financial success they achieved through Microsoft, and how they are using their wealth to tackle the bigger problems around the world through their foundation that no specific national government or world organization has the means or expertise to solve. They created and grew that quality and intensity of love, passion, and contribution in their relationship first. Their love for each other and their constant learning and growing are the primary sources of the abundance they now have. Their love for each other is the inspirational and catalytic force for their love for humanity, and that's guiding them to use their wealth in the most effective and efficient ways to assist in changing and bettering people's lives the world over. Life gives to those that give to life. The more you and your lover give your gifts to life, the more life gives back to you multiplied.

Bill and Melinda Gates are no exception to the impact love has on the lovers themselves and the world at large. The Need for contribution is a Need that is necessary, and when it's powered by love, it will provide you and your lover with a greater sense of purpose, meaning, and lasting fulfillment. You don't have to wait until you are a billionaire, as in their case, for your love and relationship to become a force for good in your family, community, and the world. The relationship you are in now is the perfect place to start giving love and contributing abundantly. Develop a deeper capacity for loving and contributing to each other and then the two of you can expand that capacity of loving and giving to your immediate family and friends. Then you eventually expand that circle of impact to your community and the world. Let your love and relationship become a force of love, caring, hope, and inspiration to the world.

Remember, everything we do for others has to begin with who we are and what we have first. You cannot contribute what you do not possess. In order to give yourself to others you must already be. It's not just with money that you can contribute to improve the lives of others. I often say a smile on your face is a great way to contribute to someone who is in need of some cheering up. But unless you feel the happiness within you first, you won't be able to even crack a smile. In other words, become that person that can make a difference in your relationship, with your family and friends, in your community, and, ultimately, in the world.

Chapter

7

The Six Stages of Relationships

Everyone wants to be in a relationship that is consistently meeting their needs and expectations, and is meaningful and fulfilling. Here is why: Human beings intuitively know and understand the importance of human connection or relationships, and that's why throughout history people came together and formed relationships. Let's remind you again of the definition and purpose of a relationship: A relationship is a place we go with the intention to meet our needs at the deepest level. The purpose of a relationship is to share and intensify human experiences and emotions.

There are six stages of relationships. The stage you consciously or out of habit decide to structure your relationship on is what will determine the kind of relationship you and your lover will have as well as the intensity of the connection, passion, love, intimacy, and fulfillment the two of you will experience. These six stages of a relationship are not just the evolutionary path every relationship goes through. They are also the reflection of the different decisions and choices individuals or their partners make as to the type and quality of relationship they want to have and be in.

Stage 1: Stage one of a relationship is the ultimate relationship everyone wishes for and dreams of having. This is a magnificent relationship in which you are insanely passionate and engaged with your partner's mind, body, and spirit. The intensity of your connection, love, passion, intimacy, and playfulness is at the highest level of ten out of out ten. This is a relationship in which you put your partner first above all else. Love is what drives you, and your love for your lover is the juiciest thing in your life. Loving your lover gives your life a deeper sense of purpose, meaning, and fulfillment. You consider yourself lucky being in love with your lover as your highest achievement. Your lover's happiness is your happiness. Because you are driven by love and your love for your lover, you see it as your responsibility for your lover to be happy, and meeting his or her needs is your primary relationship priority.

Stage 2: The second stage is the type of relationship in which the lovers love each other but the relationship lacks passion. The relationship is like two good friends that just like each other and are comfortable being with each other. This relationship has connection but depth is missing. You come first and your primary focus is on meeting your needs. It's only after you have met your needs that you try to meet your partner's. The central belief and rule in this relationship stage is that "My happiness and needs come first, your needs and what you want are secondary priorities. If you are not happy, that is not my problem but yours. If I can't meet your needs, I'm out of the relationship." This is the 50/50 type of relationship.

Stage 3: This is a relationship that is based on convenience. Both partners know in their hearts that this is not the right relationship for both of them. Neither of them is happy or fulfilled, but won't leave because of the convenience and benefits the relationship is providing. Any relationship that is based on convenience or benefits lacks dignity.

Stage 4: This is when you are in a relationship where the connection, love, and passion are at zero. You are so unhappy, so unfulfilled, and intuitively you do not see things changing, and you know the future of this relationship is going to be like the past. You are thinking about and planning your breakup. You are only waiting for the perfect time. You are looking for an opportunity to capitalize on so you can use that as justification for leaving.

Stage 5: This is where you are not in a relationship and don't even want to be in one. This usually occurs when someone has experienced dissatisfying and painful experiences and relationship fallouts, and does not want to feel that kind of pain again, so they vow never to be in a relationship again. This pain does subside for most people after some time when they come to the realization that not all women or all men make bad relationship partners and behave poorly in relationships. They learn through introspection that their mistakes came from their poor choices and selection of the people they chose to get into a relationship with. They let go of blame and the negative association they linked to relationships based on past experiences. This self-revelation leads to remarkable personal and spiritual growth. They then focus and channel their energy into becoming better and making better relationship choices in the future.

Stage 6: Stage six is the stage where you are not in a relationship but you want to be in one and are looking.

Chapter

8

Communication

Communication is one of the most essential components of any relationship, but most especially in an extraordinary relationship. In fact, there's no relationship without communication, whether it's verbal or nonverbal. It's the process in which people share experiences, thoughts, ideas, and feelings in order to fulfill their purpose of being in a relationship; to share experiences and intensify emotions.

Why is Quality Communication Important to the Life of a Relationship?

66 *It's not what you say, it's what people hear. So the meaning of your communication is the response you get.* 99

–Lucas Asu

Quality communication is as vital to the health of a relationship as oxygen is to human life. For you to have an extraordinary and magnificent relationship you **must** first make **love** the soul of your relationship, and second, make **quality communication** the **heart** of your relationship. Quality communication serves many purposes in a relationship; it establishes rapport with your lover, creates connection, heartfelt communication and understanding, builds trust, creates shared experiences, and, most importantly, deepens emotions and fulfills Needs.

Keep this little secret in mind and save yourself some serious relationships trouble: you've got to communicate every day and all the time. Without communication, you won't have a relationship. Quality communication is important not just at the beginning stages of your relationship; it's a daily requirement and it's absolutely vital every day at all stages of your relationship. If you want an extraordinary relationship, then you've got to communicate when things are great, when things are okay, and when things are terrible. Most of us have not been trained to read minds. No one can read what's in your head or what's in your heart, and your lover didn't get into a relationship to take a mind reading course from you. If you don't communicate, you don't share and if you don't share, then you don't care. The day you stop communicating is the day you have stopped being in the relationship, and it's also the day your relationship starts to die. Remember what we said before—quality communication is as vital to the health of your relationship as oxygen is vital to the health of the human body. When quality communication is heartfelt, it brings life and kindles love and passion in a relationship, and, most importantly, brings you and your lover closer as a couple to deepen your love for each other.

66 *The quality of your relationship is the quality of communication that exists between you and your lover.* 99

–Lucas Asu

What You Need to Know Before You Communicate

Most people often think and believe that it's our choice of words that determines the effect and impact of our communication, but that's not true. This may be a surprise to you as it may be questioning everything you have been taught about communication. We understand. And that's why you are reading this book to gain new insights to enhance and upgrade your communication toolbox.

Although words do play an important part in our communication process, they are not the most significant component in effective communication. And there's no better place quality communication is needed than in a relationship. So what role do words play in the quality and effectiveness of our communication? Research shows that words (what we say) are only seven percent of our communication. Yet this is what most people have been trained and taught to rely on when communicating. No wonder most relationships are so boring and dead. No wonder most people say so much but the intent of their communication is lost—they are not **heard** or **felt**. This is why they resort to **yelling** and **screaming**. This is a sign of deep frustration that "I want you to listen; I want you to see, hear, and feel what I am communicating." Most people communicate so poorly and it's evident in the communication breakdown and breakups we see in relationships.

Why is this happening at such an alarming rate? It is because people are not being heard and understood, and it's because they rely solely on words (what they say) to transport and deliver their message and meaning. NLP teaches that "**The meaning of your communication is the response you get.**" You are not reaching and connecting with your lover or the person you are communicating with because you are only using words. You want a better response and to reach and connect with them, don't you? Let's change things up so your communication can have more quality and impact, okay?

That means you need to understand there's another component of communication that's even more powerful than words, which when you start applying it, there will be a tremendous increase in the quality of your communication with your lover and anyone else you have the privilege to interact with. That component is **tonality**. Tonality represents **thirty-eight percent** of your communication. The **tone** of your **voice** when you're communicating **carries** more **emotional** impact than just your **words themselves**. It's not what you say but it's the **tone** of your voice that significantly determines the quality and effectiveness your communication will have on the person you're communicating with.

If words are only seven percent and tonality is a gigantic thirty eight percent, what then influences the quality and effectiveness of communication more than words and tonality? The answer may surprise you. It's your **physiology**! Your physiology represents a monumental **fifty-five percent** of your communication. What do we mean by physiology? By physiology we mean your posture, the gestures and the facial expressions you make, and even the way you breathe when communicating. All of these nonverbal cues have a tremendous effect on the quality and meaning of your communication to the listener more than anything else.

The key to **quality** and **heartfelt** communication is **congruency**. Congruency is when you apply words and a specific tone of voice with posture, gestures, and facial expressions all directed at conveying the meaning of what you are communicating.

Summary and Application

Use words, tonality, and physiology that are emotionally charged and emotionally rich that will light up the heart of your lover and invoke love, passion, giggles, beauty, romance, flirtatiousness, laughter, caring, comfort, warmth, playfulness, etc. You can use quality communication to create interest, attraction, deepen your connection, understanding, build trust, inspire, show caring, reassure, create certainty, and even make love. You can also use your communication to judge, criticize, find faults, put your lover down, argue and start fights, or use it to steer your relationship with your lover to a sensational destiny of love and romance. The choice is yours. Remember that the quality of your relationship is the quality of the communication that exists between you and your lover. An extraordinary relationship mandates you use all three components of communication regularly to make your communication a quality one to give life, depth, and meaning to your relationships.

Different Styles of Communication

Small Things That Make the Biggest Difference in Relationships

Most people tend to focus their attention on doing the big things in their personal lives or when in a relationship. But a careful observation of life and your relationship history will teach you that it's always the little things we don't know, or, neglect to do, even when we do know them, that most often screw up our lives. What's the biggest communication barrier that couples face in their relationship? The biggest communication barrier that destroys most relationships is the generalization and the assumption that the way I am is the way my lover is and the way I take in information and communicate is the same way my lover also takes in information and communicates. This is far from the truth.

Research and science prove that each individual has a distinct processing and communication style. There are four primary styles or modalities that people use to process information and communicate with others. Having this insight and applying the understanding can significantly enhance the quality of your relationship. And quality communication requires you to know what your preferred style is as well as your lover's. Why is this so important? It's important because most miscommunication in relationships occurs because of the lack of knowledge about how the people you are in a relationship with are wired to take in information and communicate. The greatest benefit of knowing and applying this is that your communication would have more depth and be heartfelt and your lover will feel you are the best person they've ever been in a relationship with because you just know how to communicate with him or her, and the two of you just understand each other so well.

The lack of this knowledge is the root cause of misunderstanding in most relationships. This knowledge helps to improve understanding and minimize misunderstanding to a point almost nonexistent in your relationship.

The Four Primary Styles or Modalities of Communication

There are four primary styles or modes that people use to take in information as well as communicate.

1: Visual Style of Communication: People that are primarily visual in their style of communication tend to be **louder**, speak **faster**

and make lots of **hand gestures**. This is because they process information through mental pictures and communicate in a way in which they want you to **see** what they're saying. Whenever you're having a conversation with someone who's primarily visual, they often use words such as:

Do you **see** what I am saying?

Look at what I mean.

Is it **clear?**

Picture this.

Imagine that.

Some key words visual people use: **Look, see, clear, picture, imagine, appear,** and **view.**

2: Auditory Style of Communication: A person with a primarily auditory style of communication typically communicates with a very **moderate tone,** and they are more **clear** and **precise** with the **pronunciation** of their words with special emphasis on how they **sound.**

Examples of key words auditory people use often:

Do you **hear** what I'm **saying?**

Does this **sound** good to you?

Listen.

Hear this.

Key words auditory people use often: **Say, hear, listen, sound, silence, ring a bell, tune in/out,** and all **ears.**

3: Kinesthetic Style of Communication: When someone has a primarily kinesthetic style of communication, they speak at a slower pace and have a soft tone. Their interest is based on how something feels.

Examples of key words kinesthetic people often use:

Do you **feel** what I am saying?

I have a **good feeling** about what you said to me yesterday.

Let's get a **handle** on the situation.

I have a **solid** and **concrete** idea for the program.

Key words they use include: **Feel, touch, intense, easy, solid, concrete, grasp, hard,** get a **handle,** and make **contact.**

4: Logical Style of Communication: People with a primarily logical style of communication always want to know what you are saying makes **sense.** The "why" of something is what matters. They think and speak in a very structured and logical way. Things have to be **structured, logical,** and must make **sense.** For them it's not about how something looks, sounds, or feels but rather whether it made **sense.**

Example of key words logical people often use:

Does that make **sense**?

I **know** what you mean.

Think about it.

Do you **know** that?

You are **understanding** me, right?

The **process** is going to be **easy**.

It's an **intelligent idea**.

Key words logical people use include: **Know**, **sense**, **think**, **understand**, **process**, **consider**, **decide**, and **conceive**.

Franca's clients "Mary" and "Tom" have been in a relationship for about eight years but have been married for five years now. Despite their attraction, love, and appreciation for each other, Mary and Tom were completely ignorant of each others' style of processing information and communicating. The consequence of that was their relationship suffered from misunderstanding and miscommunication. This ineffective communication led to unmet needs which brought on feelings of annoyance, anger, and frustration.

Tom's primary's communication style is visual which means he is usually loud and talks fast. On the other hand Mary's style is kinesthetic. She speaks in a soft and slow manner. Do you now see or understand where their problem is coming from? Do you hear or feel the frustration in their relationship? What is really causing this communication breakdown in their relationship? It is that unconscious assumption that "the way I am is the way my lover is and the way I take in information and communicate is the same way my lover does." Tom sees Mary to be as visual as he is and Mary feels Tom is kinesthetic as she is.

Through the coaching process, I assist them to gain that little insight into each other's communication behaviour. As small of a distinction as it may appear or sound to you, learning for the first time about each other's communication style and putting it into practice was an "aha" moment and the breakthrough both of them had been searching for. It was the turnaround their relationship needed.

Whenever Tom is speaking with his lover, Mary, he would speak in a slow and soft tone and in this way, Mary feels and is touched by what Tom is saying. He started incorporating those kinesthetic key words (feel, touch, intense, etc.) into his conversations with Mary. And when Mary is talking with Tom, she would be loud and speak in a faster tone. This enables Tom to see and picture what Mary is talking about. She began using those key visual words (see, look, picture, clear, imagine, etc.) in her conversations with Tom.

This is the magic of this science. You remember the communication mantra that we have repeated a few times? "The quality of your relationship is the quality of communication that exists between you and your lover." This is how this small distinction will give you that edge you need to make your relationship with your lover an extraordinary one.

> 66 *In life and in relationships it is the small things that make the biggest difference.* 99
>
> –Franca Navarra

By knowing and applying your new communication skills in your relationship, you'll be able to build a deeper level of rapport and connection and enter your lover's world and see what they see, hear what they hear, and really feel what they feel.

Chapter

9

The Seven Skills of Extraordinary Relationships

A core principle of NLP is modeling excellence which is the skill or ability to duplicate and apply proven concepts and strategies and reap the same results. An extraordinary relationship requires you and your lover to do the fundamental things every day to keep the bloodline of love and passion flowing abundantly in your relationship, just like breathing, eating, and drinking are necessary for you to continue to be alive. The Seven Skills of a Relationship you are about to learn will enlighten, empower, and equip you with tools and strategies to enable you to create and have that extraordinary quality relationship—a strong connection, love, passion, intimacy, and the certainty of a lasting relationship between you and your lover.

We all want to be in loving, passionate, and satisfying relationships, but we often lack the valuable skills that will provide us with the abilities and confidence to not only create such a relationship, but be able to sustain and grow that love, passion, and happiness consistently through time.

Love is going to be challenging, scary, tiresome, and boring at times. The Seven Skills of a relationship will enable you to make those occurrences be rare exceptions instead of the norm in your relationship. In this way, whatever happens to steer you and your lover off the course of love, you can handle it with confidence and purpose and redirect your love ship back on course. The norm in your relationship, if you choose to make it so, should be a relationship that's filled with playfulness and fun, heartfelt communication, and joy.

The lack of this knowledge or these skills is reflected in the alarming rate of relationship and marriage failures in our society. Information from Statistics Canada reveals that the national divorce rate is now at forty percent. In the presence of light, darkness disappears. By learning and applying these skills consistently to your relationship, you and your lover will have one of the most magnificent relationships that will be unmatched in your circle of influence.

#1: The Skill of Heartfelt Connection and a Deep Appreciation

At the centre of an extraordinary relationship is an intense heartfelt connection—a love that's pure and an appreciation that's deep between you and your lover. You got into a relationship with your lover because of how he or she makes you feel. You feel a sense of divine luck to have met and be in love with such a beautiful soul. It is this connection, this attractive, magnetic, and electrifying force that holds your love for each other together. Without this, you don't have a relationship. No relationship, especially an intimate relationship, and more so an extraordinary one, will last beyond the initial moment without a heartfelt connection.

Authenticity: This heart-to-heart connection must come from an authentic place and intention governed by love. It requires you to bring your true self and your deepest love. Authenticity demands you to be vulnerable; it means leaving all the bullshit and masking behind. It means no pretending to be something or someone other than your true self. It means you are choosing to live a life filled with love and cherish giving and receiving love. Let your actions of love speak louder than your words.

Presence is an essential component of how to create and sustain that heartfelt connection with your lover. Presence means when you are with your lover spending quality time or just relaxing and having a conversation, your whole attention, focus, and energy is in the present moment and directed to him or her. When you are fully present, it deepens connection and magnifies love.

Active Listening is also equally important. Listen to understand, not to analyze, judge or make assumptions. Appreciate and value their opinion. Listen with your heart, not with your head. Active listening strengthens the bond, the connection, and the love in a relationship. It tells your lover you value being in love with them; you value what they're sharing, and you appreciate and respect them. Active listening is critically essential in enhancing and deepening that heartfelt connection with your lover.

Connection and love don't just happen in a relationship. You must consciously and actively create and nurture them through your thoughts, emotions, communication, behaviours, and actions.

#2: Building Trust

Trust is the glue that holds a relationship together. Without trust you have no relationship. Yet, most people are completely oblivious to its importance and the consequences when this vital force is broken. The moment trust is broken by either of the lovers, the integrity of the relationship is compromised. The effect of that is that the connection, love, and passion dwindle and the attractive energy that ignites intimacy is then switched off. When trust is not rebuilt, that relationship is doomed to fail. Lack of trust is one of the primary causes of relationship failure, and any relationship can be transformed when trust is restored.

For your relationship to go beyond the level of survival or mere existence into extraordinary levels, you must build unshakable trust that nothing can ever come between you and your lover. Keep in mind that trust is not something you are entitled to, but it's something you earn by being trustworthy. You won't earn this trust by what you say; you will earn it through your behaviours and actions of love. When you create that trust in your own personality and demonstrate it through your behaviours and actions, it will then create a secure relationship and environment where both of you feel completely free to share thoughts and feelings as well as an abundance of love without any reservations.

What Destroys Trust in a Relationship?

Insecurity: When a lover is insecure about themselves, they tend to think they are not enough for their lover. This belief and perception starts to show up in many negative behaviours and accusations against the person they love. Men tend to feel insecure especially when their woman has a better job and/or makes more money than they do. Men also feel insecure when their lady is more fit and physically attractive or has a more outgoing personality.

Women tend to be more insecure about themselves particularly in regards to their bodies. When a woman is with a man who has healthy habits and takes great care of his body through regular exercise which results in having good physical looks, it often causes her to feel insecure about herself.

These unspoken insecurities women and men have do trigger the fear that **"I am not enough"** and therefore, **"I won't be loved."** It is these insecurities which create those two fears and it's those fearful emotions which then cause them to have destructive behaviours such as being suspicious, assumptive, and accusative. If you are running limiting patterns like dishonesty and disrespectfulness, they will break down trust and destroy your relationship. How can you build and sustain trust in your relationship?

Strategies for Building

The most important step you can take to create that deep level of lasting trust in your relationship is to love your lover and give him or her unconditional and abundant love. This certainty that you really love him or her from your core without a shadow of doubt is the most important step for building trust in your relationship.

Make your lover and your relationship your most important priorities. Let your family, friends, and your social world know that you love all of them, but your lover is the most important person in your life.

Walk the walk and do what you say.

Be consistent. Be consistent with your love, with your passion, and with your care. Love them even when they are in a bad mood.

Respect: Show them respect both in private and in public.

#3: The Responsibility to Fulfill Needs

The truth is everyone wants their relationships to be filled with the magic of love, passion, and, most importantly, fulfillment. The question you and your lover need to ask yourselves is whose responsibility it is to fulfill the needs of the relationship? To answer this question, let's take a look at the three levels of a relationship.

Level 1: This is a relationship in which you are completely focused on what you are getting out of the relationship. It's all about satisfying your needs and as long your needs are met and you are satisfied, that's all that matters. The other person's feelings and their needs do not count and do not matter to you. The relationship and everything in it is about you. This is parasitic love. The moment the resources to meet your needs start running low, you are gone. In street terms you are a "gold digger."

Level 2: This is the level of relationship where your focus and degree of the love you give to your lover is calculated based on what you are getting in return. The belief here is that "I will give you love and meet your needs when you give me love and meet my needs. If I don't get what I want then I won't give you what you want and need." This type of relationship is like whoring. This is also the typical 50/50 model of relationship most people have settled into.

Level 3: This is the deepest depth of love couples can dream of having in their relationship. At level three you have evolved and have embodied love as your core essence. This is the stage where you take full and total responsibility for meeting your lover's needs and happiness because you consider you and your lover to be one. You and your lover no longer consider each to be separate from the other. This is oneness of love. You love them so much and they love you equally as well. Both of you put each other first, always. You and your lover will not stop or give up until each person's needs are met and you are both happy. Contributing, giving your gifts of love, and making your lover feel loved and happy bring you the greatest joy. This is the level where you and your lover attain enchantment and experience the deepest states of love, ecstasy, and fulfillment on a consistent basis.

Only a small percentage of the world's population has evolved to embody love as their essence and have developed the capacity to love at such a depth. This is the path to having your dream; this is the path to having an extraordinary quality relationship. These relationships are legendary. Those who have allowed themselves to evolve and develop the capacity to love at this level are the ones that enjoy the greatest level of love and total abundance.

You and only you have the power to decide which of these three levels of relationship is right for you. Whichever you choose tells the world so much about who you are as a person and your overall view of life and relationships. This is also what will greatly determine your level of emptiness or fulfillment.

It is your responsibility as well as your lover's to meet and fulfill each other's needs. We recommend you re-read Chapter Three to review and remind yourself of The Six Human Needs/ The Six Pillars of a Relationship. Those Six Needs are what must be met consistently for your relationship to have that deep level of certainty of love, passion, and ecstasy.

#4: Rekindling Passion and Intimacy

We often hear from the couples we coach that they have lost their passion and romantic attraction for each other with the passage of time. These couples and clients told us that losing passion is just inevitable. As a consequence, most of their relationships and marriages have become almost like living with a roommate.

Let's get this straight—it is not natural for couples to lose passion. It is simply due to couples lowering their standards about the quality of relationship they demand of themselves and developing bad relationship habits. Some of these bad habits couples develop which dry up the passion include neglecting doing the small and daily things to keep love interesting, taking each other and the relationship for granted, not communicating their needs, not resolving the small resentments that show up, and, most importantly, not being proactive in learning new skills for rejuvenating passion and intimacy.

The Importance of Passion in a Relationship: Passion is the fire of love. Without passion, any relationship or marriage will become bland and the love the couples have and feel for each other will eventually evaporate.

In fascinating research conducted at Stony Brook University by psychologist Daniel O'Leary and his team on love and the longevity of marriage, passion or "being very intensely in love" was the dominant quality couples that have been together for ten plus years have in common. The most interesting fact about this insightful research is that passion is also the number one trait amongst couples that have been together for thirty years and more. They all attributed the longevity of their relationship or marriage to "being very intensely in love" with each other. There's something invisibly extraordinary about each of these individuals: an energy, a smile, a playfulness, or a sense of aliveness that they carry with them. It's passion. A relationship without passion is like a car with a dead engine. The car will not go anywhere and neither will your relationship.

Rekindling passion and intimacy in a relationship is an ongoing process. Don't expect to do it once and the flames and heat to remain strong forever.

The first step to rekindling passion and intimacy in your relationship is for you as well as your lover to take ownership of the loss of passion. Do this without blaming yourself or your lover. Then make a decision to develop and have a more passionate personality and way of being. Join the gym or any form of workout that will have you exercise on a regular basis. Passion is an intense energy and energy comes from motion. The more you move and exercise your whole body, the more you will revitalize your own energy and the more energy you will have to share with your lover.

Next, when you are with your lover, hold their hand and express to him or her how much you miss their emotional and physical touch and those close and intimate moments you once shared.

Then, start speaking with energy and a happy tone.

Express how grateful and lucky you are to be in love with him or her. Start kissing longer and deeper. Tell your lover you love them and touch more often.

Do little surprising things on a regular basis such as writing a note on the bathroom mirror in the morning. For example, "I love how you looked into my eyes and told me you love me and kissed me so sweetly last night." Let your lover know you really want to juice things up to have a more exciting and romantic relationship. Commit to living and having more passion in your life and in your relationship.

The amazing energy of passion is such a turn-on for both women and men. Now you know that by rekindling passion, you reignite your connection and spark for intimacy with your lover and bring the two of you back in that state of playfulness and joyous ecstasy.

#5: *Breaking Barriers and Resolving Differences*

Love is sometimes really messy. Couples sometimes do display disempowering emotions, behaviours, and habits that drive them to do silly and stupid stuff which may cause one or both pain, to be withdrawn, distance themselves, or to be emotionally wounded. Lovers can be trapped in these patterns while ignoring their effects on the relationship. These negative patterns are responsible for switching off the chemistry, love, and attraction between you and your lover. When this happens, it causes one or both of you to be turned off, shut down emotionally, and become romantically and sexually disinterested. From that moment on, the slightest thing the other person says or does triggers a storm of anger and resentment. The love and relationship they once cherished and valued begins to lose its meaning and relevance. All of these accumulate to barriers that prevent these beautiful souls from feeling and experiencing the love and affection they have for each other and defeat the purpose of why they got into a relationship in the first place. These destructive barriers must be broken and differences resolved for their hearts to be fully open and for love to begin flowing freely again.

To accomplish this task, you and your lover must want to see your relationship transformed and must take conscious, intelligent, and decisive action to break those walls and resolve differences. How can you go about doing that, you may ask?

The First Step: Get Real. Be conscious and identify the problem (emotional or behavioural patterns) and how it has been affecting your affection for your lover and the quality of the relationship.

The Next Step: Decide enough is enough and you want to change this now. Decide you won't go one more day with this way of feeling, behaving, and acting towards your lover and the relationship. Then deliberately interrupt those patterns. Stop doing whatever was corroding and eroding the connection and love between you and your lover and starving the two of you from each other's love. Break that pattern that has been keeping the two of you at an emotional distance and do the new behaviour. When you catch yourself right about to do the old behaviour, stop it, then do the new empowering alternative instead. When you interrupt an emotional or behavioural pattern enough, it will be difficult for your brain to do the same pattern again. The outcome is to break the old pattern and start doing the new empowering and fulfilling behaviour that will bring you and your lover closer and magnify the love and happiness in your relationship.

What usually gets in the way of a couple's attempts to break barriers, resolve differences, and transform their relationship is their ego and fear of being vulnerable. Do you love your ego more than your relationship or do you want to be loved? When you cherish and value your lover and your relationship more than you value your ego or your fears, you will harness the courage to break those patterns and give your relationship what is missing.

Case Study #1:

Rosaline loves their two-bedroom condo apartment to be neat and organized, but Jerry, her boyfriend of four years, has a habit of leaving things everywhere. Every day after work he would throw his socks and shoes right at the centre of the living room and his computer bag and tons of papers all over the kitchen island. Where he eats is where he leaves his plate and everything else. Even though they have a laundry basket, he throws his dirty laundry on the floor a foot away from the basket. Rosaline at first was picking them up for about two years, and then she got fed up and spoke to him about it a number of times. Nothing changed. She became angry that an intelligent adult would behave just like a two-year-old child. She even thought Jerry was doing it intentionally to disrespect her and to see her pissed off.

Step 1: Rosaline sat down with Jerry and communicated to him how much she loves him and how much she respects him. But the behaviour of throwing his dirty clothes on the floor instead of in the basket and leaving his stuff everywhere was causing her to lose respect for him and was weakening the intense connection and love she feels for him. She explained that it's causing her to be resentful. She told him she needs his support to make that change and improve their relationship.

Step 2: Interrupt the pattern. Rosaline waited for the moment Jerry opened the door, and she sprang to her feet and welcomed him with an unexpected long, sensuous kiss and then told him how she appreciates when he does those little things for her and always puts his things in the proper places. That evening while he was watching a movie and eating popcorn, at the end when he was about to get up and just go to bed, she went and cuddled with him and told him again how she's so proud of him and their relationship, and how he always supports her in keeping their apartment so neat by putting away small things such as a snack plate, a glass, tea cup, or popcorn container.

The next day while Jerry was on his way home from work, she sent him a lovely text message praising him on how sweet he is and that she feels so loved by him, and for his assistance in making sure their apartment is always neat by putting his socks, shoes, work bag work papers, and dirty clothes in the proper places. Jerry opened the door and found a handwritten card she wrote thanking him for his understanding, love, and support in doing something that matters to her so much. He placed his shoes on the shoe rack, socks in the laundry basket, and work bag in his study desk.

Case Study #2: Jacque and Nathalie: Jacque does not like to express his feelings to his wife.

One of the best ways to establish intimate connection and intensify love with your lover is through words. And this is what Nathalie craves; verbal affirmation and the expression of one's feelings and affection with words. But Jacque has a hard time expressing his feelings and sharing his affection or appreciation through words. Jacque has a somewhat quiet nature and rarely comes home and shares how his day was. To Jacque, "saying I love you all the time means devaluing its significance. It should be reserved for special occasions." Nathalie doesn't know why and Jacque does not think it's important. Is this a problem that is hurting their relationship? Yes. Nathalie's primary love strategy is that she needs to **hear** Jacque telling her he loves her in order for her to feel and believe in his love.

Step 1: Jacque and Nathalie went out on a coffee date. Nathalie softly grabbed and began rubbing her husband's hands while telling him how she desperately loves to hear him tell her he loves her and express what she means to him. She told Jacque that without him saying and expressing how much he loves her with his voice and eyes, she doesn't feel his love. She told him how important it is for her to hear his voice. Jacque opened up and confessed that he is just not used to expressing love or sharing his feelings. He feels shy, but agreed to be more expressive and sharing. He asked for his wife's support and help. She was delighted.

Step 2: During his lunch break, Jacque decided to put his commitment into action by calling his wife and telling her "I just called to let you know that I love you very much." It took him more than five minutes and some drops of sweat to make that call to his wife, who was also at work. He did it and felt relieved. He felt free. This was the first time Jacque had ever called her at work and expressed something so deeply meaningful to her. She cried tears of joy. She had indeed heard Jacque's voice in her heart. It felt so good. She felt his love.

On his way home, he was feeling anxious and excited at the same time thinking about how to tell his wife about his day and what had happened at work. He told himself that he has to keep his promise to his wife in order to make their marriage better. Nathalie had made his favourite dish. While they ate he started talking about his day and a new project he and his team are working on. Although it was unusual for Nathalie to hear her husband be so open and expressive about his day and the new project, she listened actively and asked questions which made Jacque expand and elaborate more. They ended up talking through their dinnertime. He was happy about his favourite meal his wife had made. She kissed him and thanked him for calling from work and saying those sweet words and for sharing his work day and work-related experiences.

Is it simple to break emotional or behavioural patterns? No. Is it worth it? Absolutely! And when you value love, and value your lover and your relationship, then you will do whatever it takes to break through those barriers, resolve differences, and elevate the quality of your love and relationship with your lover.

#6: Realign Values and Needs

Each of us is a unique being; each of us has acquired different values and beliefs throughout the course of our lives that now shape who we are as an individual. All of these have contributed to how we view and approach life, love, and relationships. It has also led to what each of us now values in life and in relationships. Keep this core principle in mind: People like people that are like them. When people have and share enough things in common (when they have common values), the better their rapport, the more they tend to like each other, the more easily they will relate with each other, and the greater the probability for them to establish a relationship. This means when a couple has and shares the same Values and Needs, their relationship tends to have more harmony, they tend to love each other more, they tend to be happier, and their relationship naturally lasts. Why? Because what they are getting and experiencing in their relationship matches what they value and want in a relationship. This means that their relationship is meeting their expectations of what a relationship should be and how their life should be. That is your one million dollar secret.

But when couples have opposing or conflicting Values and Needs, they tend to have more disagreements, fights, and their relationship tends to be short-lived. Even when it does last, it's often filled with misery. Why? Because what they value or what they want in a relationship is completely different from what they are getting and experiencing. Their expectation and the reality of the relationship are so distant from each other. This really means that the kind of love and the quality of relationship they have envisioned and what they actually have is drastically different. So there is a big gap between what they value and want and what they actually have and have allowed themselves to settle for in their relationships.

Whether you are considering getting into a relationship, just getting into a relationship, or you have been in a relationship for months, or a few years or decades, realigning your Values and Needs is extremely important to keep your relationship securely in love while intensifying the connection, the love, the passion, the intimacy, and growth. When Values and Needs are aligned, the quality of love and your relationship start to reflect your expectations.

When Values and Needs are not aligned, that relationship will have some hiccups and could be short-lived. In fact, the enormous challenges and high divorce rates we have in our culture accurately indicate what happens when core values and Needs are not aligned in a relationship or marriage.

How to Realign Values and Needs

Case Study #1: (Values and Needs Conflict)

Holly is thirty-three and Ben is thirty-nine, and they have been together for five years and married for one. Holly values and wants to start having children as soon as possible while Ben values travelling and seeing the world first before they start having any children. Holly believes she's at the perfect and healthiest stage to have a baby. Ben believes if they have a baby soon, they will never have the freedom to travel and explore the world.

Whose values are more important? Both are important to each of them. Both Holly and Ben have the same values and want the same things, but their prioritization is the only thing they are conflicted on. Both of them want to have children and both want to travel; their conflict (disagreement) is what should be done first. This is where alignment (coming into an agreement) will have a profound impact on the future of their relationship.

(Values and Needs Alignment)

They agreed (aligned) that they would take three months and travel the world instead of the six they had initially thought. During that time, Holly would get off her birth control pills since they would have a lot of time for romantic magic moments. If they conceive a baby while travelling, then it's just perfect. Holly was happy and Ben was happy.

Case Study #2: *(Values and Needs Conflict)*

Anna wants to return to school to further her education so she can move up the corporate ladder, have better career opportunities, and make more money. But her husband, Syed, wants both of them to stay at their current jobs to work for one more year so they can save money for a big down payment to buy their first home as well as a new car. After that, Anna can enrol for part-time courses for her Masters program.

Again, whose values are more important? Who is right and who is wrong? Neither! Each is just expressing what they believe to be more important in life and in the relationship. What will happen if these different values and Needs are not aligned? Here again we see relationship values in total conflict. This couple is not in alignment (agreement) about the order of their relationship and life's priorities.

(Values and Needs Alignment)

Anna and Syed met and worked the numbers out with the real estate agent for the type of home they desire to buy and with the car company. They also factored in what they currently had in their savings. They were in a great position. They would be able to achieve the goals of buying their first home and a new car in one year with Syed's current income, and if Anna starts a part-time job while she is in school. They agreed (aligned) that Anna doesn't have to delay her school program. She can start when the new school year begins in two months. Anna is happy and Syed is happy.

#7: Create an Exciting and Compelling Common Future

Congratulations, you made it to the last of the Seven Relationship Skills. You are one of the few that are seriously committed and are taking action to learn the skills to transform your relationship into an extraordinary one. I want to applaud you for your effort. This is what is going to give you that additional edge that ninety-five percent of the world can only wish for and sets you apart.

You must have read or heard the saying "without a vision, people perish." So it is with a relationship. Every relationship must have an exciting and compelling future. If there's none, then that relationship is doomed to fail, and if it doesn't fail completely, then it will be a mediocre relationship with a survival type of love instead of an extraordinary one. Investing in a book of this quality tells me you will never settle for something like that because you have high standards. It is human nature to want the future to be better than the past. Human beings are progress- and growth-driven creatures. They want to be growing, expanding, and making progress, and more so in their relationship. People flourish, thrive, and will be more dedicated, committed and loyal to those who offer them a more compelling future, to those that inspire them to be better people and to do better and greater things for their lives. The same is true in a relationship. Your relationship will blossom even more when you and your lover create and have an exciting and compelling common vision. It's a common future. It is not your future and he or she is just tagging along, and it is not his or her future and you are just tagging along. It's a common destiny. It is something the two of you design.

Why is This Important? A compelling common vision gives you and your lover something that is bigger than each of you, something that unifies both of you at a deeper and stronger level, and something that you look forward to knowing you are both working towards a common magnificent destiny. Your love for each other and your relationship will have a greater and deeper meaning and purpose when the two of you are committed to the same extraordinary future.

Couples are always more committed, loyal, and dedicated when they know they are part of a promising future and when they know they are active participants in shaping a beautiful future they are going to live in. An exciting and compelling common future will help to pull you and your lover through the challenges that love, relationships, and life sometimes throw at us. Without a compelling future for the relationship, lovers sometimes give up on love and the relationship easily.

Most relationships and marriages fail because they lack a compelling common future. They fail because there is nothing inspiring for a human being with intelligence to commit their energy and life to. Who wants to be in a relationship that has no compelling destiny? Nobody! No matter how much you love someone and no matter how deep that love is, for that relationship to last through time, you must create a compelling common vision.

Don't make the mistake the majority continues to make by not designing a common compelling future for their relationship, yet they want their lover to stay and continue to be in a relationship that has no destiny. Remember that "without a compelling common vision, your relationship will perish." Let's change this trend, okay? Let's take a look at an extraordinary couple that has done it in style and can act as role models.

Bill Gates and his amazing wife, Melinda, are wealthy not just in financial terms, but also when it comes to love. They are an example of an extraordinary relationship that is filled with an abundance of love. We all know the Gateses are so generous with their wealth but even more important, they are generous with their love. They have what they have and live that ultra lifestyle because early on in their relationship they took the time to create, design, and plan out their compelling common future. They did this way before their billions started pouring in and even before they appeared on the covers of *Forbes* and *Fortune*, and before the global fame in success, wealth, and philanthropy. Right at the beginning of their relationship, they decided and designed the quality of life, relationship, and marriage they wanted to have and the future they wanted to live in, and the impact they wanted their love to make on the world.

They eventually transitioned into the Bill & Melinda Gates Foundation where they are channelling their love, energy, billions of dollars, and expertise to improving and bettering people's quality of life throughout the world. It's all been made possible for them because of the map they created of what their compelling common future would be. They created a compelling common destiny because of the love they have for each other, and they wanted that love to last an eternity. They also wanted that love to be a phenomenal blessing to the world. This is why they have been directing their love, their relationship, their wealth, and themselves to serving something that is beyond the two of them, to spread love and change lives. They are living an amazing love and relationship because they first designed and created it. Their relationship is lasting because it is built on a foundation of deep love and a compelling common destiny.

What is your compelling common relationship vision?

Sources and References

- Are you the one for me

- Receiving love

- Heart of the matter

- Smart women, smart choices

- Way of the superior man

- Manifest moment to moment

- If love is a game, these are the rules.

- The ultimate relationship program

- Way you date, mate and relate

- NLP essentials

- Women can't hear what men don't say.

- Fearless loving: eight simple truths that will change your life

- Ask Barbara: the 100 most asked questions about love, sex, and relationships

- Lucas Asu: NLP & Life Coach training manual

About The Authors

Franca Navarra's Bio

Franca Navarra is a passionate lover of life, a mother to four wonderful boys, and someone who loves helping people. She started her career as an Early Childhood Educator and worked with children for 20 years. As someone who enjoys constant learning and growing, she has also received several instructor certifications in Health and Wellness and Yoga. She uses these modalities to assist individuals to live healthy lives holistically.

In 2012, Franca made a transition into the field of coaching to do something that gives her the greatest joy and would enable her to make the greatest contribution in people's lives in a more expanded and meaningful way. She is a certified Master Life Coach as well as a Master Practitioner of Neuro-Linguistic Programming (NLP). She has helped thousands of people transform their lives through one-on-one coaching, strategic family interventions, and in her workshops and seminars. Franca and her family live in Toronto, Ontario, Canada.

Lucas Asu's Bio

Lucas Asu is one of Canada's leading-edge peak performance strategists and elite results coaches. For more than half a decade now, his work has impacted the lives of thousands of people from all walks of life and backgrounds, from the top CEOs, managers, and sales professionals, to teachers, students, and parents.

Lucas is the founder of Lucas Asu Results Coaching and the author of *Success Has No Color, Only Principles*. Lucas lives in the Greater Toronto Area (GTA) in Ontario, Canada. For more information or to contact Lucas for his coaching, training, or speaking services, please visit www.lucasasu.com

NOTES

NOTES

NOTES

NOTES

NOTES

NOTES

NOTES

Made in the USA
Charleston, SC
05 February 2017